COLLUSION

By

STERLING A. KOLIBA

www.CollusionBook.com

INTRODUCTION

In this book I will lay out the evidence and the facts. You come to your own conclusion.

If this book upsets you, please feel free to use it as a coloring book.

TABLE OF CONTENTS

EVIDENCE OF COLLUSION

COLLUSION

COLLUSION

COLLUSION

COLLUSION

COLLUSION

COLLUSION

COLLUSION

COLLUSION

PROOF OF COLLUSION

COLLUSION

COLLUSION

COLLUSION

COLLUSION

COLLUSION

COLLUSION

COLLUSION

COLLUSION

COLLUSION

ACTS OF COLLUSION

COLLUSION

COLLUSION

COLLUSION

COLLUSION

COLLUSION

COLLUSION

COLLUSION

COLLUSION

Collusion by Trump's Team

COLLUSION

COLLUSION

COLLUSION

COLLUSION

COLLUSION

COLLUSION

COLLUSION

COLLUSION

COLLUSION

COLLUSION

COLLUSION BY TRUMP'S FAMILY

COLLUSION

COLLUSION

COLLUSION

COLLUSION

COLLUSION

POSSIBLE COLLUSION

COLLUSION

COLLUSION

COLLUSION

COLLUSION

COVERED UP COLLUSION

COLLUSION

COLLUSION

COLLUSION

COLLUSION

COLLUSION

THE FACTS

"We did not include evidence in our report—and I say 'our,' that's NSA, FBI, and CIA, with my office, the director of national intelligence—that had anything, that had any reflection of collusion between members of the Trump campaign and the Russians."

– Former Director of National Intelligence James Clapper. March 5, 2017

On March 8, 2017, when asked, under oath, if his original statement was still accurate, he replied "It is."

"I think he's right about characterizing the report which you all have read"

– FBI Director James Comey, March 20, 2017, when questioned, under oath, by the House Intelligence regarding the former director of national intelligence's statement that no evidence of collusion between Trump's team and Russia has been found.

"On the question of the Trump campaign conspiring with the Russians here, there is smoke, but there is no fire, at all..... There's no little campfire, there's no little candle, there's no spark. And there's a lot of people looking for it."

– Former CIA Director, Michael Morell

"There are all kinds of rumors around. There are newspaper stories, but that's not necessarily evidence"

– Senate Judiciary Committee member Senator Dianne Feinstein (Democrat – California), May 18, 2017

ABOUT THE AUTHOR

Loving husband and father

United States Marine Corps Veteran

United States Air Force Veteran

Associate of Science in Computer Networking and Cyber Security from Coastline Community College

Associate of Applied Science in Transportation from the Community College of the Air Force

Bachelor of Science in Business Administration from Argosy University

Master of Business Administration from Argosy University

First Degree Black Belt in Tae Kwon Do, World Taekwondo Federation, Kukkiwon

Certified Personal Trainer, International Sports Sciences Association

Musician

Artist

Entrepreneur

Comedian

LEARN MORE

Facebook @CollusionBook

www.CollusionBook.com

Facebook @SterlingAKoliba